THE
GROSSEST
JOKE
B⊙⊙K
EVER!

PORTABLE
PRESS

THE GROSSEST JOKE BOOK EVER

Portable Press/The Bathroom Readers' Institute
An imprint of Printers Row Publishing Group
10350 Barnes Canyon Road, Suite 100, San Diego, CA 92121
www.portablepress.com
e-mail: mail@bathroomreader.com

Printers Row Publishing Group is a division
of Readerlink Distribution Services, LLC.
The Portable Press name and logo are registered
trademarks of Readerlink Distribution Services, LLC.

All correspondence concerning the content of this book should
be addressed to Portable Press/The Bathroom Readers' Institute,
Editorial Department, at the above address.

Cover and Interior Design by Patrick Merrell

THANK YOU!
*Portable Press sincerely thanks those whose
creative efforts made this book possible.*

Gordon Javna	Jay Newman	Melinda Allman
Kim T. Griswell	Hannah Bingham	Jonathan Lopes
Trina Janssen	Peter Norton	Rusty von Dyl
Brian Boone	Aaron Guzman	Readerlink, LLC

ISBN 978-1-62686-585-3

Printed in the USA

Fourth Printing

20 19 18 17 16   4 5 6 7 8

1

'SNOT FUNNY

When is a booger not a booger?

When it's snot.

Which nut catches the most colds?

The cashew.

'SNOT FUNNY

What can you tie boogers into?

A snot.

Where does your nose go, when it gets hungry?

Booger King.

What is the difference between a booger and a plate?

The plate goes ON the table.
The booger goes UNDER the table.

What do boogers and apples have in common?

They both get picked and eaten.

What's the difference between boogers and Brussels sprouts?

Kids won't eat Brussels sprouts.

What did the booger say when the team captains were choosing players?

"Pick me! Pick me!"

What do you find in a clean nose?

Fingerprints!

What happens when you sneeze without using a tissue?

You take matters into your own hands.

'SNOT FUNNY

Why do elephants have long
fingernails?

So they can pick their trunks.

Who was hiding under
little Sammy's bed?

The boogie man.

Which king plays a bagpipe, wears a
kilt, and sneezes all the time?

The King of Snotland.

What did the booger say to
his girlfriend?

I'm stuck on you.

What's green and hangs from a tree?

Giraffe snot.

Why do farmers have noses?

So they have something to pick while they wait for their crops to grow.

Why didn't the nose make the volleyball team?

Nobody picked him.

Why shouldn't you eat boogers?

Because you don't want to spoil your dinner.

'SNOT FUNNY

Why is a haunted handkerchief scary?

Because it's covered in boo-gers.

Why don't dinosaurs pick their noses?

Because they don't want to eat
20-pound boogers.

**Why was the snowman looking for
carrots at the grocery store?**

He wanted to pick his nose.

What runs in big families?

The same thing that runs in small
families: noses.

How do you make a tissue dance?

Put a little boogy in it!

What did one booger say to the other?

You think you're funny but you're snot.

What's gross?
Finding a hair in your food.
What's grosser than gross?
Finding out it's your grandma's nose hair.

Why do gorillas have large nostrils?

Because they have fat fingers.

'SNOT FUNNY

When is a fence like a nose?

When it's a picket fence.

What did the big booger say to the little booger?

"Don't get snotty with me!"

Knock! Knock!
Who's there?
Adam's not.
Adam's not who?
Adam's not is dripping from his nose.

What do you call a booger that's wearing a helmet?

A snail.

What do you do if your nose goes on strike?

Picket.

Why did the booger cross the road?

Because he was being picked on.

Why do farmers have noses?

So they'll have something to pick in the winter.

What happened when the elephant sat on a quarter?

A booger popped out of George Washington's nose.

**What's yellow and gooey
and smells like bananas?**

Monkey snot.

Why was the nose sad?

It didn't get picked.

Knock! Knock!
Who's there?
Decode.
Decode Who?
Decode in my nose is getting worse.

What's in a ghost's nose?

Boo-gers.

2

Did you hear the joke about the fart?

It stinks.

What's the smelliest UFO?

An Unidentified Farting Object.

WHO FARTED?

Sam and Janet are taking a walk when Sam lets out a huge fart.

"Ugh," says Janet, "please stop it!"

"I would," replies Sam, "but I don't know which way it went."

How do you tell one end of a worm from the other?

Put it in a bowl of flour and wait for it to fart.

Who wears a red cape and farts in the forest?

Little Rude Riding Hood.

How does a ghost fart?

Out of its boo-ty.

What do you get if you fart on your birthday?

A birthday farty.

What happened when the kid held his breath to stop himself from burping?

He farted.

Why did the taxi driver fart?

Because his cab ran out of gas.

How is a ninja like a fart?

They're both silent but deadly.

Which Egyptian ruler farted a lot?

King Tootincoming.

What's invisible and smells like carrots?

Bunny farts!

What did the skunk say when the wind changed directions?

"It's all coming back to me now!"

How are rainbows made?

When unicorns fart.

WHO FARTED?

Why should you only put 239 beans in bean soup?

One more would make it too farty (240).

Why did the skeleton burp?

Because it didn't have the guts to fart.

What do you call a king's fart?

Noble gas.

What place should you avoid if you don't want to fart?

The gas station.

WHO FARTED?

What's the one thing a person won't do after they fart?

Admit it.

When does a boy take a bubble bath?

When he eats beans for dinner.

Why can't you smell alien farts?

Because they're out of this world.

What do you call a cat who likes to eat beans?

Puss 'n Toots.

WHO FARTED?

Two flies sit on a pile of poop.
One fly passes gas.
The other fly looks at him and says,
"Hey, do you mind? I'm eating here."

What do you call someone who doesn't
fart in public?

A private tooter.

What do you get when you mix a
matchstick and a fart?

A flamethrower.

What hits the nose when aimed
at the feet?

A fart.

WHO FARTED?

Why don't bees fart?

Their stingers might fall off.

Knock! Knock!
Who's there?
Gas.
Gas who?
Gas who just farted!

What is the sharpest thing in the world?

A fart. It goes through your pants and doesn't even leave a hole.

How are snowflakes made?

When snowmen fart.

WHO FARTED?

What do you call a professional farter?

A tutor.

What causes cold winter winds?

Frosty the Snowman eating beans.

What did the mouse say when he found his favorite cheese in cubes?

Who cut the cheese?

Did you hear about the man who went to jail for air pollution?

His farts were just that bad.

WHO FARTED?

How can you tell when a moth farts?

He flies straight for a second.

What happens when a clown farts?

It smells funny.

What happened when the kid ate baked beans before church?

He had to sit in his own pew.

What do you get when you mix beans and onions?

Tear gas.

How is a filling station like a burrito?

They both supply you with gas.

What did the underwear say to the fart?

It's time for a change.

**Why should you never fart in
an Apple store?**

Because they don't have Windows.

**Why did little Johnny Gass
win the race?**

Because nobody wanted to pass Gass.

How do you know when Grandpa's getting old?

When he farts, dust comes out.

Why did the fart get in trouble at the library?

Because he was too loud.

Where did Cinderella go to the bathroom?

In a land fart, fart away.

What's invisible and smells like bananas?

A monkey fart.

Why did the zombie eat the archer?

He wanted his bone and marrow.

Why did the zombie go to the dentist?

To improve his bite.

BR-A-A-AINS!

What is the zombie's favorite TV show?

Chomping on the Stars.

**Why did the little zombie stay home
from school?**

He was feeling rotten.

**Why didn't the zombie cross
the freeway?**

Because he didn't have the guts.

Where do zombies live?

On dead-end streets.

Zombie Kid: Mom? Why do you look so tired.

Mombie: Because I'm dead on my feet.

Why did the zombie cross the road?

To eat the chicken.

What's a zombie's favorite meal?

A Manwich.

What's black and white and dead all over?

A zombie in a tuxedo.

**What kind of engagement ring did the
zombie give his girlfriend?**

A tombstone.

**What did the zombie say when he saw
his favorite movie star?**

"I've been dying to eat you!"

When do zombies wake up?

At ate-o'clock.

Why did the zombie take a nap?

He was dead tired.

BR-A-A-AINS!

Why do zombies only date smart girls?

They just love a woman with
br-a-a-a-ins.

**When zombies break into a house,
where do they look for food?**

In the living room.

**What did the zombie say to the other
zombie who wanted to fight?**

"You wanna piece of me?"

**What kind of birds do zombies
like to eat the most?**

Cra-a-anes!

BR-A-A-AINS!

Why did the zombie sprinkle cheese powder on people's feet?

He wanted Doritoes.

Did you hear about the zombie hairdresser?

She dyed on the job.

Do dark circles around the eyes make a zombie look dead?

No, but being dead does.

What should you do if zombies surround your house?

Pray that it's Halloween.

BR-A-A-AINS!

What was the zombie kid's favorite game?

Corpse and robbers.

Why did the zombie eat the gym teacher?

He liked health food.

Why didn't the zombie finish eating the clown?

He tasted funny.

What did the zombie eat after its teeth were pulled?

The dentist.

BR-A-A-AINS!

What does a vegetarian zombie like to eat?

Gra-a-ains!

What did the zombie say to the locksmith?

You're out of lock.

Which candy do Zombie kids refuse?

Life Savers.

Why did the zombie eat a bowl of Cheerios?

He wanted to be a cereal killer.

Why did the zombie ignore his new Facebook friends?

He was busy digesting his old Facebook friends.

What do zombies like to eat at Christmas time?

Candy Ca-a-anes!

What does a zombie order at a restaurant?

The waiter.

What did the zombie say to the watchmaker?

Your time is up.

Zombie Kid: Mommy, do I have Daddy's eyes?

Mombie: Yes, dear. Now eat them before they get too cold.

What do you get when you cross a zombie with a snowman?

Frostbite.

How can you tell if a zombie is upset?

It falls to pieces.

What kind of bread do healthy zombies eat?

100 percent whole brain.

BR-A-A-AINS!

What's the zombie's favorite type
of weather?

When it ra-a-a-ains!

How did the zombie ace the math test?

It was a no-brainer.

What does a zombie like to put
on his br-a-a-ains?

Grave-y.

What's grosser than a dead zombie
in the trash can?

A dead zombie in three thrash cans.

BR-A-A-AINS!

**Why did the rotting zombie
quit teaching?**

She only had one pupil.

What do you call an undead wasp?

A zom-bee.

**Do zombies eat popcorn
with their fingers?**

No, they eat the fingers separately.

Why did the zombie go crazy?

He had lost his mind.

4

REAL STINKERS

What do you call a vegetarian
with diarrhea?

A salad shooter.

Why did the superhero flush the toilet?

It was his duty.

Why can't you hear a pterodactyl going to the bathroom?

Because the "p" is silent.

What is brown and sticky?

A stick.

Knock! Knock!
Who's there?
Butternut.
Butternut who?
Butternut step in the steaming pile of horse manure!

Who is the most constipated of all artists?

Vincent Can't Go.

Toothbrush: I hate my job.

Toilet paper: You think your job stinks? Try mine!

Why is pea soup more special than mashed potatoes?

Because anyone can mash potatoes.

What did the rooster say when he stepped in a cow pie?

Cock-a-doodle-poo!

What isn't an elephant a good pet?

It takes too long to clean the litter box.

Who lives in the toilet and fights crime with ninja powers?

The Teenage Mutant Ninja Turdles.

What vegetables belong in a toilet?

Peas.

Knock, knock.
Who's there?
Enid.
Enid who?
Enid a clean pair of underwear NOW!

What's brown and sounds like a bell?

DUNGGGGGG!

Mother: Billy! Why are you sitting on the toilet and hitting yourself on the head?

Billy: Works for ketchup!

What do you call a part-time teacher who eats beans for lunch?

A substi-toot.

Why was the sand wet?

Because the sea weed.

What is big, green, and incredibly smelly?

The Hulk's farts!

Why did Captain Kirk go into the ladies room?

He wanted to go where no man had gone before.

Your feet are so smelly your shoes hid in the closet and refused to come out.

Knock-Knock!
Who's there?
European.
European who?
European all over the floor!

Why couldn't the toilet paper cross the road?

It got stuck in a crack.

Student: May I go to the bathroom?

Teacher: Yes, but say your ABCs first.

Student: A B C D E F G H I J K L M N O Q R S T U V W X Y Z.

Teacher: Where is the P?

Student: Running down my leg.

Whaddaya call it when you go #1 before watching a movie?

A pee-quel.

Doctor: Four out of five people suffer from diarrhea.

Patient: Does that mean that one person enjoys it?

What's dumb?

Directions on toilet paper.

What's dumber than that?

Reading them.

Even dumber than that?

Reading them and learning something.

The dumbest of all?

Reading them and having to correct something that you've been doing wrong.

If you're an American outside the bathroom what are you inside the bathroom?

European!

What happens when babies eat Rice Krispies?

Snap, crackle, poop!

Did you hear the one about the elephant with diarrhea?

You should have, it's all over town.

What do you get if you cross a worm and a goat?

A dirty kid.

If there's H_2O on the inside of
a fire hydrant, what's on
the outside?

K9P.

How do website developers ask each
other where the bathroom is?

"Can you tell me the IP address?"

Why didn't anyone see the movie about
constipation?

It never came out.

What do you get when you cross a
dinosaur with a skunk?

A U-stink-asaurus.

Knock! Knock!

Who's there?

Snow.

Snow who?

Snow fun to clean an elephant's cage.

What do flies and stinky feet have in common?

You can shoe them but they never go away.

Why did the man bring a toilet to the party?

He was a party pooper.

Your toenails are so long you can cut the grass by walking barefoot.

What did the judge say when the skunk walked into the courtroom?

Odor in the court!

Thieves broke into the police station and stole all of the toilets. The police are investigating, but for now...they have nothing to go on.

What is the stinkiest dog?

The poo-dle.

Where did the rainbow go to the bathroom?

In the pot of gold.

Why did Tigger stick his head in the toilet?

He was looking for Pooh.

What do you call it when you step in alien droppings?

A close encounter of the turd kind.

Knock! Knock!
Who's there?
Distinct.
Distinct who?
Distinct of skunk is awful!

Flatulence: The emergency vehicle that picks you up after you are run over by a steamroller.

Why did the roll of toilet paper quit its job?

It was pooped.

Farting on an elevator is wrong on so many levels.

Knock, knock.
Who's there?
Sabrina.
Sabrina who?
Sabrina long time since I changed my underwear!

What did the First Mate see when he looked down the toilet?

The Captain's log.

**What do they say about a bird
in the hand?**

It can't poop on your head.

**How do you keep flies out of
the kitchen?**

Put a big pile of manure in the
living room.

Why did the fart cross the road?

It was trying to escape the stink.

**Fart: A turd honking for the
right of way.**

Did you hear about Robin Hood's toilet?

He had a Little John.

What has two legs, one wheel, and stinks?

A wheelbarrow full of manure.

What's a volcano?

A mountain with the runs.

Where do bees go to the bathroom?

The BP station.

5

DON'T EAT THAT!

Why couldn't the snake talk?

He had a frog in his throat.

What do cats eat for breakfast?

Mice Krispies.

DON'T EAT THAT!

What's green, fuzzy, and sits in a bun?

A school lunch hamburger.

What's green, fuzzy, and sits on a toilet for hours?

The kid who ate the school lunch hamburger.

What's the difference between a worm and a blueberry?

Have you ever tried eating a worm pie?

How do you keep a loaf of bread warm all day?

Let a cat sleep on it.

DON'T EAT THAT!

What did the spider order at McDonald's?

French flies.

What do you call a worm in an apple?

Teacher's pet.

How do you make a maggot stew?

Keep the maggot waiting for a couple of hours.

What's the difference between school lunch and a pair of smelly socks?

In an emergency you can eat the smelly socks.

DON'T EAT THAT!

Which cafeteria food makes you throw up?

Spew-ghetti.

Kid: Mommy! Mommy! What happened to the dry dog food Fido wouldn't eat?

Mom: Be quiet and eat your cereal.

What do you get when you cross a turkey with a centipede?

Drumsticks for everybody!

Why did the farmer eat his foot?

Because there was a corn on it.

DON'T EAT THAT!

What's a mushroom?

The place they store school lunches.

What's sticky, purple, has 16 legs, and is covered with thick, brown hair?

I don't know, but it's on your lunch tray.

How do you know that owls are smarter than chickens?

Have you ever eaten fried owl?

What do you get when you throw up Chef Boyardee canned pasta?

Barf-a-Roni.

DON'T EAT THAT!

Why didn't Batman go fishing?

Because Robin ate all the worms.

What's green, comes on a bun, and is covered in ketchup and mustard?

A hot frog.

What did the royal taster say after he drank the poisoned water?

Not much.

What's the difference between school lunch and a pile of manure?

School lunches are usually served cold.

DON'T EAT THAT!

Patient: Doctor, doctor, I've had a horrible stomachache since I ate a plate of oysters yesterday.

Doctor: Were they fresh?

Patient: I have no idea.

Doctor: How did they look when you opened the shells?

Patient: I was supposed to open the shells?

How do you make a slug drink?

Stick it in the blender.

A science teacher is teaching class. "In this bag, I have a frog, and we're going to dissect it," she says. She turns the bag over and the contents roll out: a turkey sandwich. "That's odd," she says. "I distinctly remember eating my lunch."

DON'T EAT THAT!

Whaddaya call an unsolicited e-mail that advertises processed meat?

Spam spam.

What's green and has holes in it?

Moldy Swiss cheese.

How do you do an impression of a bird?

Eat a worm.

Why do lions eat raw meat?

Because they don't know how to cook.

Foods not eaten on the *Titanic*: Life Savers and Root Beer Floats.

DON'T EAT THAT!

When is a slug a vegetable?

After you squash it.

What do pigs eat on hot days?

Slopsicles.

What's the worst thing in the school cafeteria?

The food.

Why was the sword swallower arrested?

He coughed and killed two people.

DON'T EAT THAT!

What's grosser than finding a worm in your apple?

Finding half a worm.

What did the Komodo Dragon say when it saw a flock of turkeys?

"Gobble! Gobble!"

What's the difference between a slug and a peanut butter sandwich?

Slugs don't stick to the roof of your mouth.

What tastes worse than grape jam?

Toe jam.

DON'T EAT THAT!

Why do vultures prefer bad restaurants?

The food is rotten.

What's the difference between a grasshopper and an éclair?

A grasshopper has more cream filling.

What is the difference between school lunch and a pile of slugs?

School lunch comes on a plate.

Did you hear about the dog who ate garlic?

His bark was worse than his bite.

DON'T EAT THAT!

What do ants like on their pizza?

Antchovies.

What's gray and furry on the inside and white on the outside?

A mouse sandwich.

What happens to a daddy long legs when it hides in a salad?

It becomes a daddy short legs.

What's the difference between head lice and dandruff?

Head lice is crunchier.

DON'T EAT THAT!

What happens if you eat yeast and shoe polish before bed?

You'll rise and shine in the morning.

What's the difference between a worm and a cookie?

A worm doesn't fall apart when you dunk it in milk.

Why did the boy eat the firefly?

He wanted a light snack.

What's the hardest vegetable to swallow?

The artichoke.

DON'T EAT THAT!

How do lunch ladies keep flies out of the cafeteria?

They let them taste the food.

Why should you finish your plate when you eat school lunch?

So it won't be someone else's lunch tomorrow.

How are roaches like raisins?

They both show up in oatmeal.

Mommy! Mommy! What happened to all your scabs?

Be quiet and finish your corn flakes.

DON'T EAT THAT!

Why did the dog go to school at lunchtime?

He was part of the flea lunch program.

Why did the witch send her pizza back?

They forgot the cockroaches again.

Why don't dinosaurs eat at Burger King?

They have it their way wherever they eat!

What happens if you cross a cheeseburger with a yo-yo?

After you eat it, it comes back up again.

DON'T EAT THAT!

**What do you get if you swallow
plutonium?**

Atomic ache.

Why did dinosaurs eat other dinosaurs?

Because it takes one to gnaw one.

**What do you get if you cross barf
with pasta?**

Ralph-i-oli.

**What's the best thing they've ever had
in the school cafeteria?**

A fire drill.

DON'T EAT THAT!

Can you define bacteria?

It's the rear entrance to the school cafeteria.

What happened when they threw out the school cafeteria leftovers?

The alley cats threw them back.

What do you get if you eat prune pizza?

Pizzeria.

How can you tell a mouse from spaghetti?

A mouse won't slip off your fork.

DON'T EAT THAT!

Why are frogs always so happy?

Because they eat whatever
bugs them.

How do you make a cockroach float?

Throw it in a root beer and add two
scoops of ice cream.

Why are false teeth like the stars?

Because they come out at night.

**Why did the lunch lady put her thumb
on the student's hamburger?**

She didn't want it to fall on the
floor again.

6

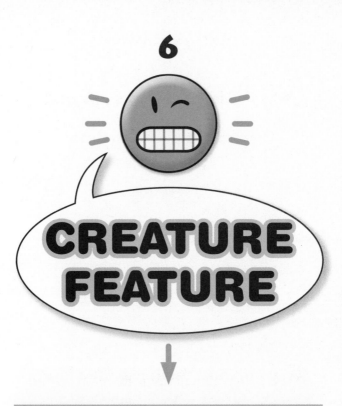

CREATURE FEATURE

What kind of fish don't swim?

Dead ones.

How much money does a skunk have?

One scent.

Why was the man fired from the zoo for feeding the penguins?

Because he fed them to the lions.

What lies on the ground 100 feet up in the air?

A dead centipede.

What's grosser than a three-headed spider with 40 eyes?

Not much.

A three-legged dog walks into an Old West saloon. He sidles up to the bar and says, "I'm looking for the man who shot my paw."

CREATURE FEATURE

Where does a bee sit?

On its bee-hind.

What do you do if you find a boa constrictor in your toilet?

Wait until it's finished.

What do you get if you cross a Rottweiler and a St. Bernard?

A dog that bites off your arm and then goes for help.

What do you call a smelly sheep?

Ewwwwwe.

What goes "snap, crackle, pop"?

A dying firefly.

What do you call fishing if you don't catch any fish?

Drowning worms.

Why couldn't the vulture fly with two dead raccoons?

The plane only allowed one carrion per passenger.

What has five legs?

A lion carrying leftovers.

CREATURE FEATURE

What's black and white and flat?

A penguin flattened by a steamroller.

What do you get when you cross a pig with a centipede?

Bacon and legs.

What do you get when you cross a T. rex with a dog?

Something that drinks out of any toilet it wants to.

**Birdy, birdy in the sky,
Dropped some white stuff in my eye.
I'm too big to whine or cry,
I'm just glad that cows don't fly!**

What has 50 legs but can't walk?

Half a centipede.

What do you get if you cross a bird with a cat?

A cat that isn't hungry anymore.

What's the last thing to go through a bug's mind when it hits the windshield?

Its backside.

Two lions played poker for a giraffe.

Why were they nervous?

The game was for high steaks.

Did you hear about the fly who put himself on the map?

He got squashed in an atlas.

What do you get when you cross a pig with a comedian?

Slopstick humor.

What goes "Eek-eek! Bang!"?

A mouse riding a firework.

Why didn't the veterinarian want to treat the toad?

She was afraid it would croak.

CREATURE FEATURE

Why did the hen wash the chick's mouth out with soap?

He was using fowl language.

What's black and white and red all over?

An exploding zebra.

What do you call a bug that has worked its way to the top?

Head lice.

What's small, grey, sucks blood, and eats cheese?

A mouse-quito.

CREATURE FEATURE

What does a triceratops sit on?

Its tricerabottom.

What's black and white and red all over?

A skunk with diaper rash.

Which reptile lives in the Emerald City?

The Lizard of Oz.

How do you stop an octopus from punching you?

Disarm it.

What's yellow, wiggly, and dangerous?

A maggot with a bad attitude.

What does a boa constrictor call its dinner date?

Dessert.

Why did the girl toss a snail out the window?

She wanted to see slime fly.

Little Skunk: Can I have a chemistry set for my birthday?

Skunk Mom: No way! You'll stink up the house!

Why did the chicken take a bath?

It smelled fowl.

What happened to the man who tried to cross a lion with a goat?

He had to get a new goat.

What do you say when you meet a toad?

Warts new?

What's black and white and green all over?

A seasick zebra.

What do you call a toothless bear?

A gummy bear.

What does a chicken say when it lays a square egg?

Ouch.

What do you call a frog with no back legs?

Unhoppy.

Why did John bring his skunk to school?

For show and smell.

7

YES WE CANNIBAL

Why do cannibals like weddings?

They get to toast the bride and groom.

What do cannibals call skateboarders?

Meals on wheels.

Did you hear about the cannibal lion with the big ego?

He had to swallow his pride.

Cannibal Kid: Dad, why can't I play with other kids?

Cannibal Dad: It's not polite to play with your food.

Why should you never upset a cannibal?

You'll end up in hot water.

How did the cannibal like his guests?

Medium well.

Cannibal Kid: Dad, I hate my math teacher.

Cannibal Dad: Then just eat your salad.

Why was the cannibal expelled from school?

She was caught buttering up the teacher.

Two explorers are walking through the forest when they get into an argument and start hitting each other. A cannibal who is spying on them yells, "Food fight!"

What's yellow and smells like people?

Cannibal barf.

Did you hear about the cannibal who thought he was a termite?

He only ate wooden legs.

What do cannibals call a bus filled with tourists?

A buffet.

Did you hear about the cannibal restaurant?

Dinner costs an arm and a leg.

Junior Cannibal: Mom! I brought a friend home for dinner.

Mommy Cannibal: Dinner is already on the table. Put your friend in the fridge and we'll have him tomorrow.

Did you hear about the cannibal who arrived late to the dinner party?

They gave him the cold shoulder.

Why did the cannibal eat the tightrope walker?

He wanted to eat a balanced diet.

What did the cannibal say to the waiter?

I'll have a large Manwich and a tossed Sally on the side.

What's a cannibal's favorite vegetable?

Human beans.

Why did the cannibal have twins in his lunch box?

Just in case he wanted seconds.

Why do cannibals make good police detectives?

Because they can really grill a suspect.

What does a cannibal eat when he's late for lunch?

Spare ribs.

What do cannibals call track stars?

Fast food.

8

THAT'S SICK

What color is a hiccup?

Burple.

What goes "Ha-Ha-Ha!" Plop?

Someone laughing their head off.

Doctor, doctor, what's the best way to avoid biting insects?

Quit biting them.

There once was a lawman named Earp,
Who threw up all over some twerp.
At the OK Corral,
He said, "Sorry, pal!
I thought it was only a burp."

Why did the fisherman go to the doctor?

He lost his herring.

What happened when the butcher backed into the meat grinder?

He got a little behind in his work.

Why did the pig go to the eye doctor?

He had pink eye.

What do you call a person who sticks their right hand in an alligator's mouth?

Lefty.

What should you do if someone rolls their eyes at you?

Pick them up and roll them right back.

What has four legs and flies?

A dead cow.

What's green and curly?

A seasick poodle.

Mom: I thought I told you to drink your medicine after your bath.

Son: Sorry, Mom. After I finished drinking the bath, I couldn't drink another drop.

What's the difference between a peach and a wound?

One bruises easily, one oozes easily.

Nurse: The new doctor is really amusing. He'll leave you in stitches.

Patient: I hope not. I only came to collect my prescription.

What's yellow, lumpy, and flies through space?

Halley's Vomit.

Patient: Doctor, doctor! My stomach hurts. I've eaten three blue billiard balls, two red billiard balls, and an orange billiard ball.

Doctor: No wonder you aren't feeling well. You aren't getting enough greens.

What was the most common illness in the Jurassic era?

Dino-sore throats!

An apple a day keeps the doctor away. An onion a day keeps everyone away!

What did the teacher say when his glass eye went down the drain?

"Oh no, I've lost another pupil."

What's the difference between a dentist and a Yankees fan?

One roots for the Yanks and the other yanks for the roots.

Doctor: What's wrong with your wife?

Husband: She thinks she's a chicken.

Doctor: How long has she been this way?

Husband: For three years.

Doctor: Why didn't you call me sooner?

Husband: We needed the eggs.

What's the cure for dandruff?

Baldness.

Why did the lion throw up after eating Abraham Lincoln?

Because it's hard to keep a good man down.

Kid: Gramps? What's more important? Your money or your health?

Gramps: Your health, kiddo. Without your health, you're a goner.

Kid: Great. So can you lend me $20?

Fight air pollution. Gargle with mouthwash!

What do you get when you combine a
drawing toy with vomit?

A Wretch-a-Sketch.

Dentist: You've got the biggest
cavity I've ever seen. You've got the
biggest cavity I've ever seen.

Patient: You didn't have to say it
twice.

Dentist: I didn't. That was an echo.

Why did the old man cover his mouth
when he sneezed?

So his teeth wouldn't fly out.

Why don't zombies eat weathermen?

They give them wind.

Where does a one-handed man shop?

In a second-hand store.

What animal always pukes after it eats?

A yak.

**A man and a woman went on the road
with their animal impressions act.
She did the sounds, and
he did...the smells.**

**Where's the best place to save
toenail clippings?**

In a nail file.

Painful Reading: *Epic Fails!* by S. Platt

What should you give a seasick hippo?

Space.

Doctor, doctor, what's good for biting fingernails?

Very sharp teeth.

Why were the barber's hands so dirty?

No one had been in for a shampoo all day.

What do you call a sick alligator?

An ill-igator.

How did the dentist become a brain surgeon?

His hand slipped.

What happened when the boy drank 8 colas?

He burped 7-up.

How do you catch dandruff?

Shake your head over a paper bag.

Doctor, doctor! How can I stop my nose from running?

Stick your foot out and trip it.

What was Beethoven doing in his grave?

Decomposing.

What's green, sticky, and smells like eucalyptus?

Koala vomit.

What's wet, stinks, and goes "thump thump thump"?

A skunk in the dryer.

What does a sick dog say?

Barf! Barf! Barf!

How do you get kids to stop biting their toenails?

Make them wear shoes.

Doctor, doctor! What should I do about my yellow teeth?

Wear a brown tie.

What do you call the first person to discover fire?

Crispy.

What's it called when you throw up on an airplane?

Jet gag.

Did you hear the one about the foot?

It's pretty corny.

Did you hear the one about the fungus?

It grows on you.

What's yellow, lumpy, and smells like a zebra?

Lion puke.

Patient: Doc! Why can't I feel my legs?

Doctor: Because I had to amputate your hands.

Why did the Mummy go to the doctor?

He was as pale as a ghost.

Who throws up more than any other little boy in the world?

Retchy Retch.

Doctor! Doctor! I swallowed a spoon!

Try to relax, and don't stir.

What's small, cuddly, and bright purple?

A koala holding its breath.

What's the best airline to get sick on?

Spew-nited Airlines.

Why did T. rex need a Band-Aid?

Because he had a dino-sore.

Patient: Doctor, my feet keep falling asleep.

Doctor: Try wearing loud socks.

Why did the toad cross the road?

To show everybody that he has guts.

9

MONSTER MASH

Why does the Mummy walk funny?

Monster wedgie.

What is Dracula's favorite fruit?

Necktarines.

Why was the blob turned away from the restaurant?

No shirt, no shoes, no service.

Why was Dracula thrown out of the butcher shop?

He was caught chop-lifting.

Why did Death carry a broom instead of a scythe?

He wanted to be the Grim Sweeper.

What do sea monsters eat?

Fish and ships.

Why wouldn't the other little monsters play with Dracula's children?

They were vampire brats.

What do you get when you cross a vampire and a gnome?

A creature that sucks blood from your kneecaps.

Junior: Mom! Everyone at school says I look like a werewolf! Am I?

Mom: Don't be silly. Now go comb your face.

Why do vampires drink blood?

Root beer makes them burp.

What does Godzilla like to spread on his toast?

Traffic jams.

Why was Frankenstein's monster furious at his creator?

Because Dr. Frankenstein overcharged him.

**I have a green nose, three red mouths, and four purple ears.
What am I?**

Monstrous!

Why did the vampire call the morgue?

To see if they delivered.

Little Monster: Mommy! Mommy! When is the pool going to be ready?

Momster: I don't know, but just keep spitting.

Why don't girls like Dracula?

He has bat breath.

Knock! Knock!

Who's there?

Dewey.

Dewey who?

Dewey have any garlic? Dracula's at the door.

How does a monster count to 13?

On his fingers.

What do you do with a green monster?

Put it in the sun until it ripens.

Boy Monster: Did you get the big red heart I sent you for Valentine's Day?

Girl Monster: Yes, I did. But it stopped beating. Can you send me another one?

Why do skeletons play the piano?

They don't have organs.

What do you call a 50-pound hornet with a slime gun?

Sir.

Why did the dragon burn down his own house?

He liked home cooking.

Why doesn't Death ever miss a phone call?

He has a grim beeper.

Why wouldn't the vampire eat his soup?

It had clotted.

What do you get if you cross a long-fanged, purple-spotted monster with a cat?

A town with no dogs.

MONSTER MASH

Why didn't Count Dracula ever shower?

He was filthy rich.

Which monster makes the worst house guest?

The Loch Mess Monster.

Nurse: What is your blood type?

Vampire: I'm not picky. Any type will do.

What's a vampire's favorite ice cream?

Veinilla.

What do little ghosts wear in the rain?

Ghoulashes!

How did the vampire hunters find Count Dracula's hidden lair?

He was coffin in his sleep.

Why did Frankenstein go to see a psychiatrist?

He had a screw loose.

What type of dogs do vampires like best?

Bloodhounds.

Why did the Kraken eat the pirate ship?

He wanted Captain Crunch for breakfast.

Which vampire liked to fly kites in thunderstorms?

Benjamin Fanglin.

Where did the skeleton keep his pet canary?

In a rib cage.

Which circus performers do vampires like best?

The jugulars.

What's a sea monster's favorite sandwich?

A sub.

10

What do you call a deer with no eyes.

No eye-deer.

What do you call a deer with no eyes
and no legs?

Still no eye-deer!

Did you hear about the magician who likes to include his siblings in his act?

Now he has two half-sisters and one half-brother.

What's the most violent job?

Chef—because they beat eggs and whip cream.

What kind of ball should you never play with?

An eyeball.

Where are dead potatoes buried?

In gravy-yards.

Why is it so hard to get a job as a sword fighter?

The competition is cutthroat.

What do you call a dog with no legs?

It doesn't matter. He won't come anyway.

What do you DO with a dog with no legs?

Take him for a drag!

What do you get when you cross an alligator and a parrot?

I don't know, but if it asks for a cracker, better give it the whole box!

Why did Mickey Mouse get hit in the head with a rock?

Because Donald ducked.

Did you hear about the stupid coyote?

He got stuck in a trap, chewed off three of his legs...and was still stuck.

What did the dumb bunny do when his computer froze?

He put it in the microwave.

Patient: Doc, you gotta help me! I broke my arm in two places!

Doctor: Try avoiding those places in the future.

How do you make a dumb bunny laugh on Tuesday?

Tell him a joke on Sunday.

Why did little Sammy feed birdseed to his cat?

Because that's where his canary was.

Patient: Doc, you gotta help me! When I drink hot chocolate I get a stabbing pain in my right eye.

Doctor: Try taking the spoon out of the cup.

Favorite Western Movie: *Gunslingers with Gas* starring Wyatt Urp

What do you call a cow that just gave birth?

Decalfinated.

Why is it dangerous to do math in the jungle?

Because if you add 4 and 4, you get ate.

Did you hear about the cow that tried to jump over a barbed-wire fence?

It was an udder disaster.

Why did half a chicken cross the road?

To get to its other side.

Patient: Doc, you gotta help me! I've become invisible!

Doctor: Sorry. I can't see you now.

What did the half-man/half-bull say before going to the store?

"I'll be back in a minotaur."

Two goldfish are sitting in a tank.

One says to the other: "You drive, I'll man the guns."

What stands in the field and says "mmmmm"?

A cow with its lips glued together.

What do you call a man with a shovel in his head?

Doug.

Why do elephants stomp on people?

They like the squishy feeling between their toes.

What do you get if you cross a bird with a fan?

Shredded tweet.

Favorite Bathroom Reading:
Fifty Yards to the Outhouse by Willy Makit; Foreword by Betty Wont

What's brown and sits on a piano bench?

Beethoven's last movement.

Jo: Our new dog is like a member of the family.

Flo: I can see the resemblance!

What was the Blob's favorite drink?

Slime-ade!

When does a car really stink?

When it's full of gas.

How a pimple keeps its shape: Zitups!

Why did the skunk cross the road?

To get to the odor side.

Suzie: Dad, are worms good to eat?

Dad: Why do you ask?

Suzie: Because there was one in your salad.

What happened when the thief fell into wet cement?

He became a hardened criminal.

Why did the toilet paper roll down the mountain?

To get to the bottom.

Knock, knock!
Who's there?
One shoe.
One shoe who?
One shoe bathe every once in awhile?

**What happened when the cat ate
Mexican jumping beans?**

Its poop jumped out of the litter box.

**What do you get when you cross a
whale with a sea slug?**

Moby ick!

Red Riding Hood's Favorite Book:
Chased by a Wolf by Claude Bottom

Dog Owner: I think my dog has ticks.
What should I do?

Veterinarian: Stop winding him.

How did the astronaut suffocate?

He farted in his spacesuit.

Book you'll never see:
Yellow River by I.P. Freely

What gave Godzilla a bellyache?

Someone he ate.

What shoots stuffing across the room?

A farting turkey.

What kind of monster can sit on the end of your finger?

The boogeyman.

Why didn't the viper viper nose?

Because the adder adder handkerchief.

Student: Do you have holes in your underwear?

Teacher: Of course not!

Student: Then how did you get your feet through them?

How are little brothers like laxatives?

They irritate the poop out of you.